Fully Insured Defined Benefit Pension Plans

Nick Paleveda MBA J.D. LL.M, CEO National Pension Partners
1/10/2015

ISBN 13-978 150 7763360

ISBN 10 150 776 3360

I. Fully Insured Defined Benefit Pension Plans

A. Introduction

The Defined Benefit Pension Plan is one of the least understood methods for accumulating assets for retirement. The Fully Insured Defined Benefit Pension Plan is even less understood, although the concept and implementation is, in fact, rather simple. Imagine if you purchase a whole life policy at age 40. At age 65, you look at the cash surrender value and you convert the value to a lifetime income or take out a lump sum amount. If you die, you have a death benefit that will provide a lifetime income to your spouse and child or a lump sum amount. -In addition, you also buy an annuity at least equal to the premium of the whole life contract each year-this is basically a Fully Insured Pension Plan. The Fully Insured Defined Benefit Pension Plan does not need an enrolled actuary to sign a schedule SB and generally will not require a Form 5500 until assets exceed $250,000. In addition, a fully insured defined benefit plan may be adopted along with a 401(k) profit sharing plan to provide an asset allocation for a small company retirement plan. This makes a fully insured plan an ideal plan for a small business owner or professional.

B. History of Fully Insured Defined Benefit Pension Plans

The law concerning insurance contract plans was written in 1974 under ERISA, the <u>Employee Retirement Income Security Act of 1974</u>. The insurance contract plans became exempt from the minimum funding rules under section 412 (now section 430). In fact, the insurance contract plans actually pre-date ERISA. These insurance contract plans were known as group annuity contracts. The first group annuity contract was issued by the Metropolitan Life Company in 1921. (1) Hence, the history of these plans may be traced back to 1921 actually pre-dating ERISA. In

1924, The Equitable Life Assurance Society of the United States announced its intention of offering a group annuity.(2) Equitable aggressively marketed these style plans in the late 1970s and 1980s to major law firms and others. These style plans used guaranteed insurance products (GICS) which provided for guaranteed interest rates as high as 19%. These plans were attacked by the IRS. However, In *Vinson & Elkins v. Commissioner,* 7 F.3d 1235 (5th Cir.1993) and *Wachtell, Lipton, Rosen & Katz v. Commissioner,* 26 F.3d 291 (2d Cir.1994), the law firms defeated the IRS attack on their defined benefit plans that used guaranteed insurance products where the IRS asserted the plans failed nondiscrimination testing. Later, when interest rates plummeted, Equitable Life (which sold high interest rate guaranteed plans) was forced to draw down from their reserves and finally had to be sold. A French consortium on insurance companies called AXA purchased Equitable. Hence today, the company is known as AXA-Equitable. In spite of these challenges, the insurance contract plans still survived and maintained their exemption from the minimum funding rules under section 412(e) (2) (B). The reason for the exemption is the plan provides the retirement benefit with a guaranteed interest rate buildup and a guaranteed lifetime income. The Life Insurance in the plan also had guaranteed cash build up for retirement and provided death benefits to participants in the plan. A traditional defined benefit plan or cash balance plan has no such guarantee. The traditional defined benefit or cash balance plan is generally funded with stocks, mutual funds and bonds which can produce disastrous results especially when the stock market declined rapidly. This happened prior to ERISA in 1974 with the famous *Studebaker-Packard* case. This case prompted Congress to enact ERISA in 1974 and form the Pension Benefit Guarantee Corporation (PBGC). However, a whole life contract and the fixed annuity contract with a guaranteed interest rate and guaranteed lifetime income do not face this result. Hence, there is no need for an enrolled actuary to determine the value of the plan, make assumptions as to interest earned on the plan, and certify the plan by filing a valuation statement under Form 5500 schedule SB. However, absent the 412/430 rules, all of the other ERISA rules apply to a Fully Insured Defined Benefit Pension plan. (3)

C. Is a Fully Insured Defined Benefit Plan a Tax Deductible Annuity?

To make life simple, look at a fixed annuity. An annuity is basically a CD issued by a life insurance company. Imagine an annuity which grows at a guaranteed compound rate of 3% (or the crediting rates of the insurance company whichever is greater).

Example"

A client buys the annuity and plans to place $100,000 a year into the annuity for 10 years at age 55. At age 65 he or she plans to retire. The annuity will grow to $1,176,865.25. This amount may be rolled over to an IRA or distributed as a lifetime income. The lifetime income would be $5,554.81 a month (using an annuity conversion rate of .00472).

In a Fully Insured Defined Benefit Plan, a client buys an annuity and funds it every year and deducts the contributions into the fixed annuity. The plan sponsor may not even need a Trust. (4) All the other rules under ERISA apply. If these rules are violated, the plan may be disqualified and loses the fully insured defined benefit plan status. For example, if the plan sponsor does not use an annuity with a "unisex rate" the plan violates *Arizona v. Norris* 463 U.S. 1073 (1983). This violation applies to all defined benefit plans and the plan sponsor not only loses fully insured defined benefit plan status, but the plan may become disqualified. For example, the plan sponsor funds the plan with a variable unisex annuity. The plan may become a 'traditional defined benefit plan" which requires a schedule SB. For example, if you have one common law employee, the plan may require a PBGC filing. For example, if the plan has two common law employees, the plan is subject to nondiscrimination testing under section 401(a)(4), section 410(b) and 401(a)(26). The IRS rules relating to qualified plans are extensive. (5)

D. Fully Insured Defined Benefit Pension Plans

The Fully Insured Defined Benefit Pension plan has the ability to withstand the changing velocity of the market which may create inadvertent underfunded or overfunded plans-(6) This is due to the guaranteed rates placed into the insurance or annuity contracts. For this reason, a Fully Insured Defined Benefit Pension plan can be a superior retirement plan, with less regulation then a traditional defined benefit plan and even more tax efficient then a 401(k) plan. The Fully Insured Defined Benefit Pension plan may be more tax efficient due to the lack of payroll taxes being removed from the contributions to the plan. For example, in a 401(k), the employer pays the employee after removing 15.3% of pay for social security and Medicare taxes-then the employee makes the contribution to the 401(k). In a Fully Insured Defined Benefit Pension Plan, the employer makes a contribution directly to the plan. No social security tax. No Medicare tax. Basically the Fully Insured Defined Benefit Pension Plan eliminated a 15.3% "load". Abusive Life Insurance had been a problem with certain insurance contract plans and certain 401(k) plans as well. Fortunately, in fact, most of the life insurance policies actually worked well in a Fully Insured Defined Benefit Pension Plan. However, many years ago, 5 insurance companies created "suppressed cash value policies" with the intent to spring them later outside of the plan. These plans were an attempt to abuse or "game" the tax system of the United States. Gaming the system does not work well in ERISA. Fortunately the vast majority of insurance companies actually did not play this game and instead issued Life insurance policies that had high cash values in these plans. These are policies that are paid up at age 62 or 65 a/k/a LPL 65 or LPL 62. To be safe, the plan administrator should follow <u>Rev. Rule 74-307</u> and the death benefit is set at 100X monthly earnings. In some cases a plan administrator may follow the 66 2/3d rule. However, the 66 2/3d rule is not a "rule". This is a method of funding is based on a letter written from Phoenix Home Life to the Commissioner which was not even a Private Letter Ruling. In fact it was informal guidance. (7). Under <u>Revenue Ruling 74-307</u>, if you fund a plan with 50% life and 50% annuity and the small business owner cannot make the full contribution by year 2, the plan may fall out of compliance. No reduction can take place in the Life contract, as the premiums are fixed by contract. The plan cannot reduce the annuity, as a 74-307 violation would take place where more than 50% of the contributions would be for the life insurance. Hence the 100X monthly earnings is a safer contribution to the plan. Third, adjustments now can be made to the annuity although you may lose fully insured status and become a traditional defined benefit plan as you no longer provide "level annual funding". (8)

E. Conclusion

An advisor should look at Fully Insured Defined Benefit Pension Plans along with 401(k) plans. Abusive 401(k) plans as well as certain abusive insurance contract plans are "listed transactions" but these policies have been withdrawn from the marketplace. (9) If the plan sponsor does not use abusive policies, the plan sponsor does not need to fill out a Form 8886. Although there is much discussion today on the internet about "abusive insurance contract plans", it does not mean all insurance contract plans are abusive. In addition, annuity only insurance contract plans are not listed transactions and have performed well relative to the market over the last decade (see schedule A, fn 10).

On July 6, 2012, President Obama signed the <u>Moving Ahead for Progress in the 21st Century Act</u> a/k/a MAP-21 which contained three provisions relating to defined benefit plans. The act provided for adjustments in the interest rate assumptions beginning in 2012 which will result in employers contributing less money into their pension by allowing higher interest rate assumptions. The act also increased the PBGC premium from $35.00 per participant to $42.00 in 2013 and $49.00 in 2014. Variable rate premiums also increased. Finally, the act allowed transfers of excess pension assets to fund future retiree health benefits and transfer of excess pension assets for retiree life insurance. This Act could have a positive effect on overfunding DB plans under section 404(o). Perhaps an overfunded pension plan could use the overfunded amounts to provide for post- retirement medical benefits under 401(h). This Act is relatively new and some regulations and guidance has not been promulgated as of this date.

II. FLOOR-OFFSET PLANS

A. Introduction

"When I use a word, Humpty Dumpty said in a rather scornful tone," it means just what I choose it to mean-neither more nor less". "The question is', said Alice, "Whether you can make words mean so many different things." "the question is", said Humpty Dumpty," which is to be master-that's all."-Lewis Carroll, through the Looking Glass.

Floor Offset plans have been recently on the Docket of the Supreme Court of the United States. Floor- Offset plans generally allow plan participants to receive a "floor benefit" of $x per month for life from a defined benefit plan. The floor- offset plan states to the extent another plan such as the profit sharing plan can support this benefit, contributions by the company or plan sponsor are "offset" by the amount accrued in the profit sharing plan. This may reduce the overall cost of sponsoring this type of defined benefit plan. The first cases decided by the circuit courts were *Lunn v. Montgomery Ward & Co.*, 166 F.3d 880 (7th Cir. 1999); *Pritchard v. Rainfair, Inc.*, 945 F.2d 185, 187-90 (7th Cir. 1991) and *Holliday v. Xerox Corp.*, 732 F.2d 548 (6th Cir. 1984); Recent Supreme Court cases have given plan administrators a bit more breathing room when making administrative decisions on qualified pension plans for their clients. The Supreme Court has taken a realistic view in the area of plan administration. The Supreme court is discouraging litigation in this area by allowing the lower courts to reform trust instruments to prevent non intended results. Three recent cases have addressed pension plans resulting in saving plan sponsors billions of dollars due to mistakes made by actuaries and attorneys. These plans involved:

A. The Xerox plan in the case *Conkright v. Frommert* 130 S.Ct. 1640, 176 L.Ed. 2d 469, (2010).

B. The Verizon plan in the case *Young v. Verizon* 615 F.3d 808 (2010), Cert denied 10-765, 10-911 (2011), and

C. The CIGNA plan in the case *CIGNA v. Amara* 131 S.Ct. 1866 (2011).

Only the *Verizon* plan did not reach the Supreme Court as the court declined to hear the case.

This "cert denied" in essence upheld the lower court decision not to allow *Verizon* to be responsible for $1.7 Billion dollars in additional benefits due to an attorney error. In deciding these three cases, the following three questions were addressed.

1. When can an administrator not take into account the time value of money?

2. When can a plan document have a formula that states the greater of A and B, but really mean the greater of A or B?

3. When does a summary plan description only provide a "summary" which may not really be an accurate description of a plan?

The answer is when the Supreme Court of the United States allows "reformation" of documents due to "scrivener's errors".

B. Pension Plans

A pension plan is a defined benefit plan or a retirement plan that promises to provide a lifetime income to the employees or participants of the plan once they reach normal retirement age, I.R.C. section 401(a). In some cases, the employees are given an option of a lifetime income or a lump sum amount which then can be rolled over to their IRA. The employees are provided a summary plan description which gives the employee an indication of the benefits of the program. The employee is generally not responsible for contributions, the investment return, the compliance, or the benefits of the program as it is an employer sponsored plan. The risk of the plan is placed on the plan sponsor. In the last twenty years, plan sponsors have decided in many cases to shift the risk back to the employees by adopting a defined contribution plan. In some cases, plan sponsors have tried to mitigate some of the risk in a defined benefit plan by converting the plan into a cash balance plan where the employee will receive the balance in their account, not a percentage of pay based on their final salary or their highest three year salary or their average annual salary. Private employers, for the most part have converted theses plans to cash balance plans to mitigate their exposure to declining interest rate returns and investment returns. These cash balance conversions have been the subject of extensive litigation. Congress attempted to curtail this litigation in The Pension Protection Act of 2006, which barred Age Discrimination in Employment (ADEA) claims, however the Act was prospective and any existing claims were left to the Courts to decide. The Second Circuit Court of Appeals has barred claims such against pension plans due to lack of standing of participants to sue pension plan administrators *see Fisher v. Penn Traffic Co.*, 319 Fed. Appx. 34 (summary order unpublished opinion not precedential 2d Cir. 2009), however the Supreme Court has not ruled concerning the issues in the Fischer case but tends to grant standing and certainly tends to grant standing in a 401(k) plans *see LaRue v. De Wolff, Boberg & Associates, Inc.* 552 U.S. 248 (2008)

C. Supreme Court Cases

1. Conkright v. Frommert 130 S.Ct. 1640, 176 L.Ed. 2d 469, (2010)

The first case recently decided by the Supreme Court allowed an actuary not to take into account the time value of money as "deference" was granted to the plan administrator. The *Conkright* case involved the interpretation of the Xerox pension plan where the plan administrator did not take into account the "time value of money". In *Conkright,* Justice Roberts gave the majority opinion and stated:

"People make mistakes. Even administrators of ERISA plans. That should come as no surprise, given that the employee retirement Income security Act of 1974 is "an enormously complex and detailed statute", *Mertens v. Hewitt Associates,* 508 U.S. 248,262 (1992), and the plans that administrators must construe can be lengthy and complicated."

Conkright involved the Xerox pension plan where the employees received lump sum distributions of benefits they had earned up to that point and were later rehired. The dispute concerned how to account for the past distributions when calculating their current benefits. The plan administrator used a "phantom account" method. In the decisions below, the District Court granted summary judgment in favor of the plan administrator applying a "deferential standard of review" to the plan administrator's interpretation. The Second Circuit vacated citing the standard was "unreasonable" and the respondents were not notified that the 'phantom account" method would be used. On remand, the District Court considered other approaches including not accounting for the time value of money. The District Court this time did not apply a deferential standard of review, instead found the "plan to be ambiguous" and allowed the approach that did not take into account the time value of money. The Second Circuit now affirmed holding that the District Court was correct not to apply a deferential standard and the decision on the merits was not an abuse of discretion.

Two questions were raised before the Supreme Court.

1. Should "deference" be granted to the plan administrator interpretation of the plan?

2. Whether the Court of appeals properly granted deference to the District Court on the Merits.

The Supreme Court had already addressed the standard of reviewing ERISA plans in *Firestone Tire and Rubber v. Brunch*, 489 U.S. 101 (1989). If ERISA did not directly address the matter, the court would look to "trust law". If the trust document gives the trustee the power to construe disputed or doubtful terms, the trustee's interpretation will not be disturbed if it is "reasonable". The *Firestone* approach was expanded in *Metropolitan Life Ins. Co. v. Glenn* 544 U.S.___(2008). In *Metropolitan Life,* a plan administrator was operating under a conflict of interest. This is quite common as the plan administrator usually answers to the corporation executives, not the employees. In *Metropolitan Life*, trust law was applied and discretionary authority is granted even in the face of a conflict. However in *Conkright*, the Second Circuit had carved out an exception to this "deferential standard." The Second Circuit held that a court need not apply a 'deferential standard" where the administrator had previously construed the same plan terms and the Court found a construction to violate ERISA. This approach was rejected by the U.S. Supreme Court. The Supreme Court stated:

"…we refuse to create an exception to *Firestone* deference…recognizing that ERISA law was already complicated enough without adding "special procedural or evidentiary rules" to the mix. …..If a conflict of interest does not strip a plan administrator of deference…it is difficult to see why a single honest mistake would require a different result."

Absent a showing of bad faith, the Supreme Court will uphold the decision by the administrator of the plan. Part of this rationale is given in the opinion by Justice Roberts.

"Congress enacted ERISA to ensure that employees would receive the benefits they had earned, but Congress did not require employers to establish benefit plans in the first place…… Congress sought to create a system that is not so complex that administrative cost, or litigation expenses, unduly discourages employers from offering ERISA plans in the first place."

Deference allows predictability as an employer can rely on the expertise of a plan administrator rather than worry about unexpected and inaccurate plan interpretations that might result from de novo judicial review. Both the respondents and the *amici* briefs concurred that "deference" to plan administrators served these important purposes, but they argued that "deference" is less important once a plan administrator had issued an interpretation of a plan found to be "unreasonable". The Supreme Court would not accept this clearly not wanting to carve out an exception. In *Conkright v. Frommett*, the actuary did not account for the "time value of money" when benefits were being projected-just an "honest mistake".

2. Young v. Verizon, 615 F.3d 808 (2010), Cert denied 10-765, 10-911 (2011)

In 2011, the Supreme Court declined to review and let stand the lower court decision that prevented *Verizon* from funding an additional 1.7 Billion dollars in additional pension benefits because of an "attorney mistake" in a cash balance conversion. Recall in *Conkright*, for the administrator and actuary to fund benefits, all the actuary needed to do was not take into account the "time value of money". In *Young v. Verizon*, 615 F.3d 808 (2010) cert denied 10-765, 10-911 (2011) the employees had other issues and argued:

 1. That a discount rate should have been the PBGC interest rate not 120% of the interest rate, and;

2. The multiplication was done once rather than twice as stated in the plan document.

The plan document clearly had an error, otherwise known as a "scrivener's error".

The Lower Court held that upon determining the language was a mistake, the committee should have sought to reform the plan document in court: subject to de novo judicial review. The important part of the defendant's case was asking for reformation of the plan document. Even though Verizon was negligent, this was not a bar to reformation. The plan was reformed and the discount rate chosen by the administrator was used and the multiplication was done once-not twice, perhaps to avoid "unjust enrichment". The remainder of the litigation involves who will pay the attorney's fees. Attorney's fees are awarded under ERISA 502 (g) (10 which provide:

"In any action under this title....by a participant, beneficiary, or fiduciary, the court may allow a reasonable attorney's fee and cost of action to either party."

The Supreme Court in *Hardt v. Reliance Standard Life Ins. Co.*, 130 S. Ct. 2149 (2010), held that a court may award fees under ERISA when the claimant has achieved "some degree of success on the merits" 130 S.Ct.at 2152. A "trivial success on the merits" or a "purely procedural victory" will not suffice." *id.* at 2158. The U.S. District Court ruled in *Verizon* that the Court would consider awarding fees for time attributable to the Transition factor issue, or multiplication factor issue which if left to stand could have resulted in a Billion dollar mistake.

3. Cigna Corp v. Amara, 161 S. Ct. 1866, (2011), May 16, 2011.

Next the Supreme Court listened to *Cigna Corp v. Amara*, 161 S. Ct. 1866, (2011). In *CIGNA,* the employer had established a traditional defined benefit plan with a lifetime income to the employees based on salary and length of service. A new plan was established in 1998 which is known as a cash balance plan where the benefits will be only the value of the account and CIGNA will make contributions to the account each year. Then CIGNA sent a notice to the employees explaining how generous they were transitioning the plan from a traditional defined benefit to a cash balance plan. The notice, also known as a 204(h) notice, was sent to the employees and the notice misrepresented the benefits. The misrepresentation was clearly a vain attempt by management to show the employees that a change to a cash balance plan was in the best interest of the employees when clearly it was not in the employee's best interest. In reality, management did not do a good job in promoting the benefits of a cash balance plan which are:

(1) A faster vesting schedule, 3 years as opposed to six and

(2) Portability to a new company.

Instead, management stated and touted the new plan would "significantly enhance" its retirement program" and would produce "the same benefit security" with "steadier benefit growth". Record E-503 (Exh.98). However, in fact, the company saved $10 million annually by converting the traditional plan to a cash balance plan. The U.S. District Court stated the notice had defects and cause the employees "likely harm". The District Court then ordered CIGNA to pay benefits accordingly finding authority in ERISA 502(a) (1) (B) which authorized a plan participant or beneficiary to bring a civil action to recover benefits due under the terms of the plan. The Second Circuit Court of Appeals affirmed.

When this issued reached the Supreme Court of the United States argued on November 30, 2010 and decided May 16th 2011, the Supreme Court held that 502(a)(1)(B) did not give the District Court authority to reform the CIGNA plan. Instead relief is authorized by 502(a) (20 which allow a participant, beneficiary or fiduciary to redress violations of ERISA or the plan terms. The U.S. Supreme Court *vacated the judgment* against CIGNA and remanding the case back to the District Court. Justice Breyer stated,

"Because the District Court has not determined if an appropriate remedy may be imposed under 502(a) (3), we must vacate the judgment below and remand this case with further proceedings consistent with this opinion."

Part of the problem in the CIGNA case, is the plan benefits due to the conversion were "oversold' to the employees. In November 1997 the newsletter stated that the new plan would "significantly enhance" its retirement program and would produce an "overall improvement in retirement benefits and would provide the same benefit security with steadier benefit growth." In fact, according to the actuaries, the company would save about $10 million dollars annually by converting the plan. This is partially due to the fact under a traditional plan as salaries increase, benefits can rise dramatically especially where the benefits are based on "final pay". It is also due to the fact as participants get older, the contributions may not have kept up with the benefit promised, and partially due to interest rates declining, where the actuarial assumptions account for higher interest rates. For example, if interest rates are 10%, to provide a $40,000 benefit without reducing principal, one would need $400,000. If interest rates decline to 5%, one would now need $800,000 to provide the same benefit. In a cash balance plan, this risk goes away as the participant is only entitled to what is in his account and whatever lifetime income it would buy.

4. Can you Trust your Summary Plan Description?

ERISA section 102(a) and 104(b) require a plan administrator to provide beneficiaries with summary plan descriptions and with summaries of material modifications:

"Written in a manner calculated to be understood by the average plan participant….. that are sufficiently accurate and comprehensive to reasonable apprise such participants and beneficiaries of their rights and obligations under the plan." 29 U.S.C. 1022(a), 1024 (b).

The Summary plan description in CIGNA stated the employees would receive the greater of A+B. The plan document, however, stated the employees would receive the greater of A or B. The District Court ordered and enjoined the CIGNA plan to reform its records and to reflect that all class members now receive A+B benefits. The Second Circuit issued a brief summary order affirmed the District Court's decision. On Appeal to the U.S. Supreme Court, CIGNA argued that 502(a) (1) (B) does not in fact authorize the district Court to enter into this type of relief. The U.S. Supreme Court agreed. According to the Supreme Court, 502(a) (1) (B) grants a court the power to enforce the terms of the plan but not "change them". The Supreme Court ruled that a summary document provide communications with beneficiaries about the plan *but they do not constitute the terms of the plan.* However, section 502(a) (3) is different. That provision allows a participant, beneficiary or fiduciary to obtain "other appropriate equitable relief." (Or in English this is where the Courts can change the terms of the plan).

The First question is whether the District Court may reform the terms of the plan in order to remedy the false or misleading information CIGNA provided in the Summary plan description? Historically, Courts of equity could only void or enforce but not reform a contract, *Bradford v.*

Union Bank of Tenn., 13 How 57, 66 (1852); <u>J. Eaton, Handbook of Equity Jurisprudence</u> p.618 (1901).

Second, the District Courts remedy held that CIGNA would not take from employee's benefits it had already promised. This would take place if the participants received A, not the greater of A+B or a formula which is the greater of A or B.

Third, the District Court required the administrator to pay already retired beneficiaries money owed to them under the plan as reformed.

Equity Courts have the power to grant monetary relief. The real question then, according to the Supreme Court, became how the failure to provide proper summary information in violation of the statute injured employees even if they did not act in reliance on the summary documents. To obtain relief, the participant must show that the violation injured him or her. In this case, the Supreme Court asked that a showing of "actual harm" take place and the case was remanded for further proceedings.

Conclusion

In conclusion, plan administrators can now breathe a sigh of relief. However if you are an employee, you need to see the plan document-not the summary plan description. If you find your plan has structural problems, the IRS has allowed corrections to take place through the <u>Employer Plan Compliance Resolution System</u> program a/k/a EPCRS. If the plan cannot be corrected through EPCRS, and you are in litigation, you may be able to have the court "reform" the trust under 502(a) (3) to account for errors that were made in the plan document. These errors could have devastating effect on the plan sponsor, however the Supreme Court has adopted what appears to be a pragmatic view to solving problems faced by qualified plan administrators. It also appears that a 412(e) (3) plan could adopt a floor-offset approach.

III. Cross Tested Pension Plans

A. Introduction

In the world of enrolled actuaries, cross-tested retirement plans have been the ubiquitous choice for small business owner, physician, attorney and other professionals. In the <u>Defined Benefit Answer Book 4th edition</u> (Panel Publishing), the enrolled actuary G. Neff McGhie, spends an entire chapter analyzing various plan options and comes to the conclusion that the cross-tested plan gives the business owner the largest contribution relative to a group of employees while still maintaining compliance under the nondiscrimination rules under section 401(a) (4). Cross-tested plans have another advantage. The cross-tested plan is protected from creditors under Federal law. Other asset protection techniques have failed recently. The Alaska self-settled spendthrift trust failed to protect the business owner in *In Re Mortensen*, Case No. A09-00565-DMD, Adv. No. A09-90036-DMD. United States Bankruptcy Court, D. Alaska (2012). Offshore trust have problems as business owners have been held in contempt of court and in many cases sent to prison, *see SEC v. Bilzerian*, 112 F.2d 12 (D.C. Cir. 2000); and *In Re Stephan Jay Lawrence* 251 B.R. 630 (Dist. Ct. Fla. 2000). Hence, Cross Tested Retirement Plans may be the Future of Tax and Asset Protection for the Small Business Owner.

B. Types of Retirement Plans

1. The 401(k) Plan

A 401(k) plan is a plan to defer salary also known as an elective deferral plan. 401(k) plans was passed into legislation in 1978 effective for the year 1980. Today, these plans are the most popular plans in the United States, yet the most tax inefficient. The reasons these plans are tax inefficient is that social security taxes and Medicare taxes are taken out first before the assets are placed into the plan. In a cross tested plan, these taxes are not paid as the contributions generally come from employer contributions not employee contributions.

The reason the plans are popular is the 401(k) plan contributions generally come from the *employee* salary deferral and not from the company or *employer*. The burden of funding is placed on the *employee*, not on the corporation or *employer*.

The additional taxes on a 401(k) can add up to 15.3%.

The 401(k) plan has advantages relative to an IRA. A business owner may contribute more to the 401(k) plan than an IRA. For example, a business owner may contribute $18,000, otherwise known as the 402(g) limit, to the 401(k) as opposed to $6,000 to an IRA. A Business owner may add an additional $5,500 to a 401(k) if he is over age 50. Loans are also available in a 401(k) as well as hardship withdrawals. In service withdrawals are also available to a 401(k). The disadvantages of a 401(k) as opposed to an IRA are the administration cost can be higher as ADP and ACP test must be completed each year. Loans and withdrawals can add additional fees. There is a penalty of 10% if withdrawals are made for participants who are under age 59 ½ and they do not met any of the exceptions under section 72(t). The stock market may make corrections prior to retirement, and the account may not be sufficient for retirement.

The IRS has certain guidelines in establishing a 401(k) plan. The basic qualification rules are found in section 401(a). The rules are also set forth in section 401(k) and the timing of establishing a plan is set out in Rev. Ruling 81-114. In many cases, a company will establish a "safe harbor" plan and contribute 3% of pay to the employees to satisfy nondiscrimination testing. These plans must be established by October 1, Non-safe harbor plans may be established by December 31st. A plan established on December 31st may receive a deduction under section

404 for employer contributions until the filing of the corporate return including extensions and a deferral under 401(k) for employee contributions if made before the end of the year. The plan must be in writing and communicated to the employees.

2. Types of 401(k) Plans

There are several different types of 401(k) plans. There is the Traditional 401(k) plan, the Safe harbor 401(k) plan and the SIMPLE 401(k) plan. You may also have a ROTH provision in the plan document along with provisions that allow loans, in service withdrawals etc. The plan document may be a prototype, a volume submitter or even a custom plan.

a. Traditional 401(k) Plans

In a traditional 401(k) plan, an employee can elect to defer up to $18,000 of their salary which can represent 100% of their salary. The employee is 100% vested in the amounts deferred as they are considered a form of vested compensation. If the employer makes a contribution to the plan, such as a profit sharing contribution, the employer contribution can be subject to a vesting schedule which may be a 6 year graded vesting schedule or a 3 year cliff vesting schedule. In many cases, the employees who are NHCEs (Non-highly Compensated Employees-by definition compensation less than $120,000 and not a 5% shareholder or greater) do not defer and only the HCEs (by definition compensation greater than $120,000 or greater than 5% shareholder) defer which creates a plan failure of meeting the nondiscrimination rules and the contributions are then refunded back to the employees or a QNEC (Qualified Non Elective Contribution) contribution must be made. Due to these plan failures, which will not be known until the end of the year, many companies elect to set up a 'safe harbor 401k.

b. Safe Harbor 401(k)

A safe harbor plan must provide for employer contributions which are fully vested. These contributions usually consist of a 3% of pay contribution or a "match". The 3% of pay contribution used to satisfy the safe harbor cannot be used to pass the "gateway test" to "cross-test" a plan. The "gateway test" under 1.401(a)(4) basically mandates a 7.5% contribution to the non- highly compensated employees who are in the profit sharing plan to allow a defined benefit plan for the highly compensated employees. These safe harbor plans must make an election by October 1.

c. SIMPLE 401(k)

A SIMPLE 401(k) is not subject to nondiscrimination testing. This plan must have fewer than 100 employees who receive at least $5,000 in compensation to be a participant in the plan. If another plan is found along with a SIMPLE plan, the SIMPLE plan is terminated and the assets are refunded. No penalty will apply according to ASPPA technical tip 71 (2000). Administration is basically following the terms of the plan document.

In all 401(k) plans, the assets are held in a trust and are in the custody of an asset manager who is also a fiduciary of the plan. A trustee or business owner who selects the platform and asset manager may be held liable for selecting the asset manager, *see LaRue v. Dewolff, Boberg et.al* 128 S.Ct. 1020 (2008) This Supreme Court of the United States case granted standing to plan participants that file lawsuits against plan administrators who is generally the business owner.

A 401(k) plan requires information to be sent to the employees known as a Summary Plan Description or SPD. The SPD is created with the plan document and must be given to all plan participants. The SPD is not the plan and if found in conflict with the plan, the plan document controls, *see Cigna v. Amara,* 161 S.Ct. 1866 (2011). A plan in operation must follow rules concerning contributions, vesting, nondiscrimination testing, investment options, fiduciaries, government reports, distribution options and compliance. Eligibility and Participation are also important. A Participant is eligible if they are over age 21, however if the plan document allows a younger age may be used to become a participant. For example, your document can allow participants who are age 18 to become eligible in the plan. The plan document cannot exclude participants who are over age 21. Union employees or nonresidents may also be excluded from eligibility in a plan.

A plan can also require one year of service before an employee becomes eligible. A plan can also use a shorter period such as all employees are immediately eligible. A plan may provide for two year eligibility, however in this case, the employees are now 100% vested in company contributions. A plan may provide that at least 1000 hours of work must be done to become eligible to participate in a plan. The plan document may have a lower amount of hours, such as 700 or 500 but cannot state 2000 hours or 1100 hours to become eligible. Contributions to a 401(k) elective deferral are limited by what is known as the 402(g) limit which this year is $18,000. Excess contributions may be carried over into a future year without penalty, but cannot be deducted in the year contributed.

A SIMPLE 401(k) provides a match of up to 3% of compensation or a non-elective contribution of 2% of pay. The maximum amount that can be deferred by the employees into a SIMPLE 401k plan is $12,500 by the employees. The total contribution to a plan is 100% of compensation up to a maximum of $53,000. If the participant is over age 50, the participant can add another $2,500.

3. Combining Fully Insured Pensions with a 401(k) plan under Section 404 (a) (7)

The combined plan limit under 404(a) (7) applies if the participant receives contributions from more than one plan. This limit does not apply if the defined benefit plan is covered by the PBGC (Pension Benefit Guarantee Corporation). The limit does apply if the defined benefit plan is not covered by the PBGC and the maximum contribution to the profit sharing plan is reduced from 25% of pay to 6% of pay, with a maximum contribution of $53,000. However, the participant will never reach the $53,000 limit as the maximum considered compensation is $260,000 and 6% x $260,000 is $15,600. This limit does not affect the elective deferrals, but does limit the amount of employer contributions the participant can receive. The participant can work for many corporations, but the limit is $18,000 per person under 402(g).

This section is also known as the "combined plan limitation". The new law was enacted in the Pension Protection Act of 2006 to encourage pension plans to become fully funded. However, some plans are not covered by the PBGC such as "professional service providers" with less than 25 employees *see* <u>ERISA 4021 (13).</u>

If the defined benefit plan is not covered by the PBGC, the tax deductible contribution to a profit sharing plan will be limited to 6% of pay. This can create problems in a cross tested DB/DC plan where 7.5% of pay is needed to pass the gateway test and perhaps additional contributions are needed to pass 401(a)-4 independently. The maximum deduction of 6% of pay also uses a maximum considered compensation of $260,000 under 401(a) (17).

PBGC coverage is not elective. A plan is covered by the PBGC according to the rules of the PBGC or they are not covered. The definition of "professional service providers" leaves open a question of medical technicians. You may obtain a letter ruling from the PBGC if you are not clear about the status of PBGC coverage.

4. Other Rules:

a. Vesting

The employer contributions are vested over time only if the employee remains employed by the corporation. Vesting can be graded over 6 years or 100% after 3 years. These schedules are deemed equivalent. Employee funds are always 100% vested to the employee. Employer funds may be forfeited back to the plan if the employee quits or is terminated. If the plan is terminated, the employee becomes 100% vested in the plan.

b. Beneficiary of the plan

A 401(k) may have a trust as a beneficiary. A trust must meet certain requirements. The trust must be valid under state law, irrevocable at death, the beneficiaries must be reasonably identifiable and the trustee of the plan provided with a copy which has a list of all the beneficiaries and an agreement that if the trust is amended, the trustee of the plan will receive the amendments within a reasonable time. The documentation must be provided by October 31 of the year following the year of the owner's death.

c. Nondiscrimination testing

Nondiscrimination testing involves setting up two distinct identifiable classes of employees.

1. The Highly compensated employee a/k/a/ HCE which by definition is an employee who has received more than $120,000 in compensation or is a 5% or greater shareholder.

2. The Non-highly compensated employee a/k/a/ NHCE who makes less than $120,000.

Testing compares either (1) Contributions or (2) benefits, between the two groups. These tests are found in 1.401(a)-4. In a defined contribution plan, the test generally is based on a percentage of contributions to a plan. For example, each employee received 10% of pay to a plan. One employee received $20,000 based on his $200,000 pay another received $2,000 based on his $20,000 pay. In a defined benefit plan, tests are based on a percentage of pay at normal retirement age as a form of benefit. For example, one employee receives $20,000 a year for life and another $2,000 a year for life. However, the employee who is to receive $20,000 a year for life will retire in 5 years and the funding is significant where the employee who is to receive $2,000 a year for life is to retire in 45 years and the funding is very small. Cross testing is taking the funding rules of defined benefit plans and applying them to a defined contribution plan to pass nondiscrimination testing.

5. 401(k) Plan Investing

Investment options are important. Today, many insurance companies and mutual fund companies have platforms that are used to invest qualified plan funds and keep required records and valuation of the funds. A person who sells financial products to a plan may be a fiduciary to a plan was PTE 84-24 may not apply and the advisor becomes an "inadvertent fiduciary". Several cases have reached the courts regarding this issue including *Reich v. Lancaster* 55 F.3d 1034 (5th Cir. 1995), and *Consolidated Beef Industries v. New York Life,* 949 F.2d 960 (8th Cir.1991). Generally, a fiduciary is a person who has discretionary control of the plan funds or provides investment advice to the plan for a fee or has discretionary authority over the assets.
These rules are in a constant flux as to who is a fiduciary as the Department of Labor attempts to expand jurisdiction over the advisors to the plan.

a. Penalty for withdrawals 72(t)

If a participant removes funds out of a plan prior to age 59 ½, the participant may be subject to an additional 10% tax on top of the income tax. The penalty does have several exceptions such as uniform systematic withdrawals through life expectancy, purchase of a home etc. The penalty is 25% if the funds come from a SIMPLE IRA. After age 59 ½ but prior to age 70 ½ funds may be withdrawn without the penalty, only ordinary income taxes.

Early distributions that are not subject to this penalty include tax free distributions from Coverdell education savings accounts, tax free scholarships, Pell grants, employer provided assistance and veteran assistance. First time homebuyers where the maximum amount is 410,000 and the amount is used to pay acquisition cost before 120 days. The residence must be the main house of the person, the spouse, child, or grandparent. The exception to the penalty applies if the homebuyer did not own a home during a 2 year period prior to the purchase. A qualified reservist may also be exempt if called into active duty after September 11, 2001 and on active duty more than 179 days. The distributions may be from a 401(k) or 403(b) plans if made from the time of active call to close of the active duty period.

b. 401(k) Plans

A plan trustee must provide a fidelity bond. In June, 2012, new disclosure rules under DOL rule 408(b) concerning the commissions and fees associated with the plan will go into effect. A participant is entitled to receive summary plan descriptions, individual benefit statements and a summary of material modifications to a plan. Reporting is on a form 5500 or a 5500EZ in a one participant plan. The reporting is made electronically through EFAST. If a plan has not filed or filed late, this may be done through the DVFCP known as the Delinquent Voluntary Filer Compliance Program, usually with a $750.00 penalty.

c. Lawsuits and Asset Protection

Today there are over 1,168,000 attorneys in the United States. The small business owner or professional could be a target of an unjust suit which can cost them everything as they near retirement age. Cross-tested plans have been made exempt from these lawsuits by the Bankruptcy Restructuring Act of 2005. Thus, the Cross-tested plan is not only a good method for saving taxes, but also a method for protecting the asset from creditor claims.

Qualified plans are generally exempt from bankruptcy, IRAs are exempt but with limits of one million dollars unless state exemptions are greater. These changes clarified the Supreme Court case *Patterson v. Shumate*. The summary of the <u>Bankruptcy Abuse and Consumer Protection Act of 2005</u> stated:

Section 224 -

Permits an individual debtor to exempt from the property of the bankrupt estate certain tax-exempt retirement funds that have not been obligated in connection with any extension of credit. Excepts from an automatic stay certain income withheld from debtor's wages for the benefit of an employer-sponsored pension, profit-sharing, stock bonus, or other specified plan. Excepts from a discharge in bankruptcy amounts owed by the debtor to certain plans established under the Internal Revenue Code. Sets an asset limitation on debtor's retirement funds that debtor may exempt from the estate in bankruptcy.

Section 225 -

Sets forth criteria for excluding certain education individual retirement accounts from the property of the bankruptcy estate if the designated beneficiary is the debtor's child or grandchild.

6. Cross Testing

Cross testing is a method used to meet nondiscrimination rules. The formula for EBAR (Employee Benefit Accrual Rates) is important to known in creating a Cross Tested 401(k) profit sharing plan otherwise known as a new comparability plan. When performing a test for nondiscrimination, the elective deferrals are not considered as they represent "employee contributions". The test is measured on the "Employer contributions". A defined contribution plan such as a 401(k) profits sharing plan uses employee benefit accrual rates as opposed to employee normal accrual rates and most valuable accrual rates which are used in a defined benefit plan. Hence the name EBAR!

Example: John age 60 has his employer contributes $10,000 into an annuity that will give him 5% for 5 years. Sue age 25 has her employer contributes $2,000 one time into an annuity at 5% for 40 years. The plan has a normal retirement age of 65.

After 5 years, John will have a balance of $12,763 and Sue will have a balance of $14,080. Sue came out ahead as she had a longer time to invest the funds even though her contribution is lower. Sue is a NHCE and John is a HCE. The formula to test a plan is basically:

Amount invested * (1+i) ^

i= interest rate

^= amount of years.

Two ways to test a DC plan.

1. On an allocation basis: Regs. 1.401(a)-(4)-2
2. On a "benefits basis" Regs. 1.401(a)-(4)-8(b).

Testing on an allocation basis is simple, testing on a benefits basis there are two rules that must be complied with.

1. The "Gateway rule" under Reg. 1.401(a) (4)-(8) (b) (1). In effect January 1, 2002 this can start at 5% of pay to a maximum of 7.5% of pay.
2. The "equivalent accrual rule" found in Reg. 1.401(a) (4)-(8) (b) (2).

There also is a special rule for target benefits found in Reg. 1.401(a) (4)-(8) (b) (3).

a. Future value or lump sum

The first step is to calculate the future value or what the lump sum will be in a plan where a series of deposits will be made into a plan. These series of deposits with an assumed interest rate will determine a "lump sum" amount. Treasury regulation 1.401(a) (4)-(B) (2) (II) (b) refers to this as "Normalization". Normalization is a lumps sum amount at retirement.

The second step is to convert the Lump Sum into a lifetime income. The math is easy, divide the lump sum amount by the annuity purchase rate. In English, how much of a lifetime income will this sump sum give me?

Annuity Purchase Rates

What is an annuity purchase rate (also known as an annuity conversion rate)? If a participant gives and insurance company one million dollars, what will the insurance company give the participant as income for life at age 65 where if the participant dies; the insurance company will keep the lump sum? Two factors come into play, the interest rate assumption and the mortality assumption. The lifetime income can be.

A. $100,000

B. $80,000

C. $60,000

The APR is found in regulation 1.401(a) (4)-12. If you use a standard mortality table, the annuity rate is usually expressed as an amount that would be received monthly. For example, if you give the insurance company $1,000 the insurance company will pay the participant $6.00 per month. This amount will need to be multiplied by 12 to annualize the rate for testing purposes. 6 x12=72 or a 7.2% return.

The third step is to take the benefit and divide it by the individual 414(s) compensation to arrive at an EBAR. Some actuaries have called this the equivalent benefit accrual rate, but the regulations never use the term EBAR. Each employee in a plan will have an EBAR and each employee in a plan is either a HCE or a NHCE.

Example

John age 60 makes $230,000 a year. The plan contributes $46,000 a year to John or 20% of pay. Sue makes $20,000 a year. The plan contributes $1,000 a year or 5% of pay. It appears impossible to pass nondiscrimination testing on the basis of allocation as John receives $46,000 to Sue $1,000. It looks bad a percentage of pay $20% as opposed to 5%. How do you pass nondiscrimination testing?

Look at "equivalent benefits".

First calculate John's EBAR. The APR is 115.39 based on the 1983 IAF table of 8.5% (46,000* 1.085^5) *12/115.39/230,000=3.128.

John has an EBAR of 3.128.

Second, calculate Sue's EBAR. $(1{,}000 * 1.085^{22})/115.39/20{,}000 = 3.129$.

Sue has an EBAR of 3.129.

The HCE and NHCE are placed into a "rate group". John has a lower EBAR 3.128 then Sue 3.129 and the plan is deemed nondiscriminatory. In the past and actuary would fill out your schedule Q demo 5-6 and wait for the IRS to give you a favorable opinion letter.

John received $46,000 and Sue received $1,000 and the plan is nondiscriminatory as to "benefits". Why is this possible? First, the age of the participants, John is 17 years older than Sue. Second, the compensation is different, $230,000 a year as opposed to $20,000. The maximum considered compensation for testing purposes today is $245,000. Finally the interest rate assumption used of 8.5%. If you used a rate of 7.5% a different result would take place.

John $(46{,}000 * 1.075^5) * 12/115.39/230{,}000 = 2.986$

Sue $(1{,}000 * 1.075^{22}) * 12/115.39/20{,}000 = 2.553$

The plan fails testing.

John's EBAR is now greater than Sue and you fail testing. But what happens if John was born in the latter half of the year and is really close to age 61 with 4 years to retire. If you use the age nearest birthday in testing, the EBAR is lower. Is Deference given to the administrator today under *Conkright v. Frommett* for plan testing?

Lower EBAR. $(46{,}000 * 1.085^4) * 12/115.39/230{,}000 = 2.883$ results when a shorter time frame is used for retirement.

The General Test

Employer contributions are considered nondiscriminatory in a defined contribution plan by following a "uniform allocation method" or the "general test" which is found in defined benefit plans, see Treas. Regs. 1.401(a) (4)-2. The name "cross testing" is derived by using the defined benefit rules to pass testing in a defined contribution plan. The employer provided benefits under a defined benefit plan are considered nondiscriminatory if each "rate group" under a plan satisfies 410(b). A "rate group" consists of each HCE and all other employees who have a "normal accrual rate greater than the HCE and also a most valuable accrual rate greater than the HCE.

The example found in Reg. 1.401(a) (4)-3(c)-4 provides a demonstration of rate group testing. A company has 1100 employees employee 1-1000 are considered nonhighly compensated employees ad employees 1-100 are considered highly compensated employees. There are 100 rate groups as there are 100 highly compensated employees.

A calculation is performed to determine the normal accrual rate and the most valuable accrual rate for each group.

Assuming Rate Groups are as follows:

NHCE 1-100 has an NAR of 1.0 and a MVAR of 1.40,

NHCE101-500 has a NAR of 1.5 and a MVAR of 3.0

NHCE 501-750 has a NAR of 2.0 and MVAR of 2.65 and

NHCE 750-1000 has a NAR of 2.3 and a MVAR of 2.80.

Next the highly compensated employees

H1-50 has a NAR of 1.5 and a MVAR of 2.0.

HCE 51-100 have an NAR of 2.0 and MVAR of 2.65.

Rate group H1-H50 satisfies the ratio percentage test as 90% of the NHCWEs have a higher NAR and MVAR then H1-50. Only N1-100 has a lower rate and we needed 70% to pass.

But what about H51-100? H51-100 is lower than all NHCE groups except N501-750 and N750-100. H51 passes the ratio percentage test-why?

H51-100 represents 50% of the HCEs and N501-1000 represents 50% of the NHCEs. 50/50=100% and we need 70% to pass.

Example 2 provides the same facts except H96 has an MVAR of 3.6%. No other employee that is an NHCE has this high rate. The plan would pass by treating H96 as not benefitting as this group constitutes less than 5% of the HCEs. The commissioner may determine the plan is nondiscriminatory based on these facts and circumstances.

Hated example 2 gives a 5% "fudge factor" along with discretion to the commissioner. Actuaries hate facts and circumstances test as this test cannot be quantified.

NAR-Normal Accrual Rate.

What is a "normal accrual rate"?

In the regulations it is the increase in the employee's accrued benefit during the measurement period divided by the employees testing service expressed as a dollar amount or average annual compensation.-Basically an EBAR.

MVAR- Most Valuable Accrual Rate

What is MVAR-same definition except it is the increase in the "most valuable optional" form of payment. The optional form of payment is determined by calculating the normalized QJSA associated with the accrued benefit. If the plan provides a QSUP, the MVAR must also take into account the QSUPP in conjunction with the QJSA.

In cross testing a profit sharing plan, there usually is no QSUPP or QJSA to take into account and hence no MVAR. MVAR in defined benefit plans includes early retirement subsidies, early retirement benefits, etc. The measurement period can be the current plan year, the current plan year and all prior years or the current plan year and all prior and future plan years.

Secret Formula

Step 1. Lump sum at NRA or

Contribution* $(1+i)$ ^

Step 2.

(Lump sum/APR)*12=annual benefit.

Step 3. Benefit /compensation=EBAR

Cross- tested plan designs takes into account calculating EBARs, passing the gateway and general test.

DATA SUBMITTED BY DR. SMITH: Retirement through a cross tested plan.

SMITH MEDICAL CENSUS

Participant Name	Compensation	Age
Dr. Smith	$200,000	55
Dr. Jones	$200,000	50
Amy Zucker	$40,000	45
Beth Unizker	$30,000	40
Charles Taylor	$25,000	35
Will Stewart	$20,000	30
David Sopk	$20,000	25
Ely Richards	$20,000	21

RESULTS FOR DR. SMITH

SMITH MEDICAL CUSTOM CARVE-OUT PLAN

Participant Name	401(k) Plan	DB Plan	DBEBAR	DCEBAR	401a4EBAR
Amy Zucker	—	$3,239	2.00	—	2.00
Beth Unizker	—	$1,580	2.00	—	2.00
Charles Taylor	—	$897	2.00	—	2.00
David Sopk	$1,000	—	—	8.66	8.66
Dr. Jones	$10,000	—	—	1.13	1.13
Dr. Smith	—	$152,416	8.00	—	8.00
Ely Richards	$1,000	—	—	8.66	8.66
Will Stewart	—	$503	2.00	—	2.00

Conclusion:

Cross Tested plans provide asset protection and tax benefits. Contributions are simply determined on a "benefits basis" as opposed to a contribution basis. The population of baby boomers need to fund more for retirement, a cross tested plan can be an ideal solution as they are generally older and more highly compensated and will achieve larger contributions on a benefits basis. There is not much guidance in performing cross testing with a 412(e) (3) plan and a profit sharing plan. No regulations or examples have been promulgated by the IRS at the time of this writing which places the administrator in a position of using a "reasonable" standard. Perhaps the Supreme Court will give "deference to the administrator" in performing this task.

ABOUT THE AUTHOR:

Nick Paleveda MBA J.D. LL.M, Adjunct Professor, Graduate Tax Program, Northeastern University, received his B.A. in 1977 and M.B.A. degree in 1979 from the University of South Florida. Mr. Paleveda received his J.D from the University of Miami in 1982. Next, Mr. Paleveda attended the University of Denver and received his Master of Laws in Taxation in 1984. During the summer, Mr. Paleveda attended programs in Oxford University for law in England and international business at Harvard University in the U.S. In 1984 he was admitted to practice law in the State of Florida, admitted before the U.S. Tax Court, and admitted before the 11th Circuit Court of Appeals. Mr. Paleveda founded the law firm Hampton, Paleveda, Murphy, Cody and Levy in 1984. Later, Mr. Paleveda was hired to work for Mutual Benefit Life. While at Mutual Benefit Life, Mr. Paleveda conducted over 1,000 Advanced Tax and Estate Planning Seminars throughout the U.S. in almost every major city. Mr. Paleveda' client list included; the founder of Dunkin Donuts, the President of Phillip Morris, the President of Kimberly-Clarke, the founding family of Coca-Cola and others. In 1993 Mr. Paleveda returned to law practice at the firm of Paleveda and Rome in Atlanta. In 1997 Mr. Paleveda became a contributing author for "The Life Insurance Answer Book for Qualified Plans and Estate Planning" (1997) published by Panel Publishing now a division of ASPEN publishing. In 1997, Mr. Paleveda was appointed the Adjunct Professor for Retirement Planning for the College for Financial Planning at Oglethorpe University in Atlanta. In 2001 Mr. Paleveda became a CEO for a pension administration firm in Seattle Washington. In 2006, Mr. Paleveda became CEO for an executive compensation consulting firm in Bellingham Washington and in 2010, the President of National Pension Partners. Mr. Paleveda is an avid chess and trivia player. Mr. Paleveda is a USCF chess master and the Florida State Chess Champion in 1977, 1978 and 1994. He was a top 10 player in Chess nationally in high school and placed 7th at the National Chess Competition in college after winning the Southern region. He currently plays for the State of Washington Chess Team in matches against British Columbia and Oregon. In Trivia, his Team won the Whatcom County Championship two years in a row. (One year with the help of Ken Jennings as his teammate). Mr. Paleveda is also a member of Infinity International Society a top 99.63% society. In 2009, Mr. Paleveda was admitted to practice before the 9th Circuit Court of Appeals and the Supreme Court of the United States. In 2011, Mr. Paleveda became an Adjunct Professor for the Masters in Taxation Program at Northeastern University, Boston. In 2011 Mr. Paleveda presented "401(k) plans and Cross Testing" for the University of Denver CPE CPA program. Mr. Paleveda presented "Tax Strategies" for the Washington Society of CPAs and The Florida Institute of CPAs. In 2012 in Las Vegas Mr. Paleveda presented "Tax Strategies" for the National Institute of Pension Administrators annual conference in Las Vegas. Mr. Paleveda is a member of the Florida Bar and American Bar Association. The opinions expressed are only the author's opinions and not the opinions of Northeastern University or its affiliates. He can be reached at Nick@nationalpensions.com

IRS Circular 230 Disclaimer: To ensure compliance with IRS Circular 230, any U.S. federal tax advice provided in this communication is not intended or written to be used, and it cannot be used by the recipient or any other taxpayer (i) for the purpose of avoiding tax penalties that may be imposed on the recipient or any other taxpayer, or (ii) in promoting, marketing or recommending to another party a partnership or other entity, investment plan, arrangement or other transaction addressed herein. *The views expressed are the opinions of the author and not of National Pension Partners, Northeastern University or its affiliates.*

Endnotes:

(1) *See* Kenneth Black Jr., <u>Group Annuities</u> (Philadelphia: University of Pennsylvania Press, 1955 p.9).

(2) Ibid p. 11

(3) T.D. 7706 issued on July 15,1980 addressed issues relating to insurance contract plans which provided these plan have "level premiums" T.D. 7762 January 23, 1981 allows the use of variable annuities in a 401(j) plan. This rule also limits that cash value of a 412(i) plan that allows direct distribution of the annuity contract. Fortunately T.D. 7762 was Repealed by 1983.

(4) S*ee* Reg. 1.401-8(b) (iii) (b). You do not even need to file a form 5500 until the assets exceed $250,000-see Instructions to form 5500. For those who are reading this article, the footnotes are important.

(5) Nick Paleveda MBA J.D. LL.M, <u>412(i) Defined Benefit Plans</u>, A.R.I.S. 2005

(6) *See* Paleveda and Podleski, "Small Retirement Plans face funding Dilemma", *Journal of Accountancy*, May 2009.

(7) Revenue Ruling 74-307, as clarified by the November 8, 1979, letter from Winfield C. Burley of the IRS to Robert G. Chipkin at Phoenix Mutual Life Insurance Company (Chipkin Letter), provides that the maximum amount that may be used to pay premiums for whole life insurance products in a defined benefit pension plan is 66 2/3% of the theoretical reserve under the Individual Level Premium (ILP) funding method. If greater, the insured death benefit may be as high as 100 times the projected monthly benefit.

(8) "Premium payments may be considered to be level even though items such as experience gains and dividends are applied against premiums, Reg. 1,412(i)-1(b)(2)(ii).

(9) The first "listed transaction" under Revenue Ruling 90-105 was a 401(k) plan requiring a Form 8886.

(10) SCHEDULE A

Comparison of Pension Annuity and the S&P 500 Year	Contribution	Running Total Pension Annuity	Rate	Contribution	Running Total S&P 500	S+P 500 Rate
2000	$100,000	$105,550	5.55%	$100,000	$90,860	-9.10%
2001	$100,000	$217,575	5.85%	$100,000	$168,202	-11.89%
2002	$100,000	$332,997	4.85%	$100,000	$208,130	-22.10%
2003	$100,000	$449,018	3.70%	$100,000	$397,542	28.69%
2004	$100,000	$568,233	3.50%	$100,000	$551,710	10.88%
2005	$100,000	$692,623	3.65%	$100,000	$683,709	4.91%
2006	$100,000	$824,372	4.00%	$100,000	$907,456	15.79%
2007	$100,000	$964,535	4.35%	$100,000	$1,062,745	5.49%
2008	$100,000	$1,112,439	4.50%	$100,000	$669,529	-37.00%
2009	$100,000	$1,245,812	3.00%	$100,000	$943,606	26.46%
2010	$100,000	$1,386,186	3.00%	$100,000	$1,169,986	12.11%
2011	$100,000	$1,427,777	3.00%	$100,000	$1,169,986	0.00%